MINISTRY OF PUBLIC BUILDING AND WORKS

# Pendennis
# + St. Mawes
# Castles

*LONDON*

HER MAJESTY'S STATIONERY OFFICE

1963

*First published 1963*

*Fourth impression 1970*

SBN 11 670309 1

# Contents

*Henry VIII, the founder – by Holbein*    *Copyright H.M. The Queen*

# Pendennis
# + St. Mawes Castles

## Historical introduction

In 1538 England lay in peril of invasion. Reconciliation had been reached between the Emperor Charles the Fifth, ruler of Spain, the Netherlands, and much of Germany, and Francis the First of France, whose territorial rivalry it was the aim of English diplomacy to keep warm. Henry the Eighth had been excommunicated and Pope Paul the Third preached a crusade against him who bore comparison with the Turk. The Pope doubtless hoped that many of Henry's subjects would welcome their deliverance as soon as an expedition set foot in England.

So the King based his reply on two courses of action. He began to remove the last possible rivals to his throne; and he set about strengthening the fortification of all his coastline facing the Continent. It was a prosperous time for the Royal treasury, scores of monasteries being dissolved by Act of Parliament and their revenues seized; and for eight years large sums, ample materials, and a strong labour force were devoted to creating new castles and blockhouses or to modernising fortresses of older type all along the coast from Hull to Milford Haven. This work begun in 1538 in face of a "pretensed invasion", as a document of 1540 puts it, was the most extensive scheme of coastal defence undertaken in England until the last century.

Part of this scheme was the pair of castles that still guard the mile-wide entrance to the inlet of Carrick Roads east of Falmouth. These are the ancient monuments Pendennis and St. Mawes Castles. They were not the first in the programme to be built, for Kent and the Isle of Wight were more nearly threatened as likely landing places than the estuaries of Humber or Fal; but as exhibits of a phase they are among the best remaining.

There is a tradition that they were designed by one styled in contemporary records Stephen the Almayne (*i.e.* the German), who was

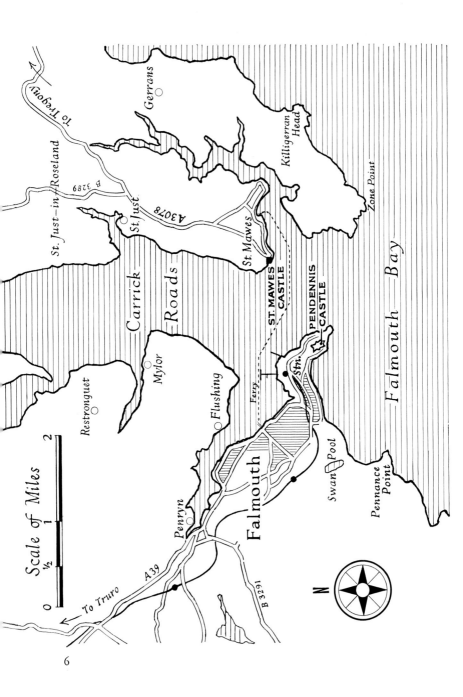

6

probably Stefan von Haschenperg, from Moravia, a military architect known to have been employed by Henry the Eighth. But Dr. Pevsner states that there is no documentary connexion between this man and these two structures. Cornishmen will repeat a tale that Henry came to see how they were progressing; again there is no record. It is now accepted that Pendennis was started by the autumn of 1539 and St. Mawes by the spring of 1540; and that both were finished by 1543. Pendennis must at all times have been somewhat the larger.

The castles are akin in being obviously planned as strongholds for kingly or national purposes. Half a century having passed since the Wars of the Roses, they are utterly unlike fortified dwellings of the feudal age when private armies moved between skirmish and siege. The prevalence they proclaim is of gunpowder, not of the arrow. Technically they show in their outworks how the round tower, so typical a feature of the Middle Ages, was being superseded by other forms.

Where the castles are almost exact opposites is in their situations. Pendennis was placed on the highest point of a promontory, while St. Mawes is overtopped by the hill behind it. No one has put this antithesis more happily than Carew in his *Survey of Cornwall* carried out in the last year of the first Queen Elizabeth: "St. Mawes lieth lower and better to annoy shipping, but Pendennis standeth higher and stronger to defend itself". Whether the Tudors thus planned wisely or ill was never tested during their dynasty; but a consequence was seen when in 1646 the Civil War came to Cornwall, bringing these castles for the only time into bright historical light. Their fates were as contrasted as their sites: St. Mawes yielded without a shot, whereas Pendennis defied the forces of Parliament for five months, as will be narrated.

Before the First Great War both buildings had been in use as barracks, married quarters, and training grounds for militia. When war was declared they were included in the system of coastal defence. In 1920 they became ancient monuments and were handed over to the Commissioners of Works (now the Ministry of Public Building and Works). The Army resumed possession in 1939 and the castles were reopened to the public in 1946. For Pendennis that date was significant, marking the third centenary of the chief event that happened there.

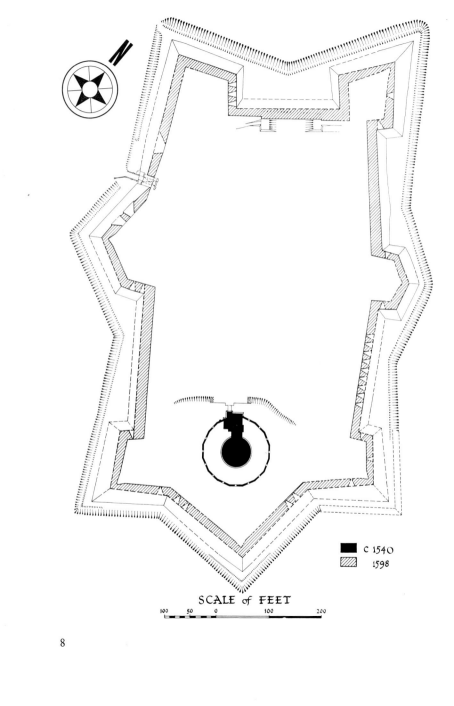

N

C 1540
1598

SCALE of FEET
100    50    0    100    200

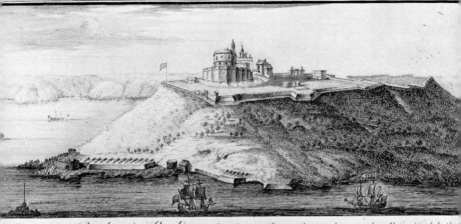

*Impression by S. and N. Buck in* 1734

# Pendennis Castle

This name is doubtless the equivalent of Pen-Dinas in Welsh, and implies that the castle stands on the site of an ancient fortification. On a 9-foot map of the south-west coast made about 1540, a prehistoric cliff castle seems to be indicated. Tradition says the Vikings had settled here too.

Only the innermost portion of the castle, consisting of keep and curtain wall, was raised from 1539 onwards by Henry the Eighth, to withstand assaults by small enemy or pirate fleets as probably he foresaw. The big enclosure and its bastions are Elizabethan. In 1583 and 1591, before and after the Spanish Armada, the Queen reviewed her father's work to guard against full-scale invasion. She also authorised musters of men from parishes around. But it must be remembered that war began rather than ended with the Armada; and the great transformation at Pendennis took place as the result of another scare. Four Spanish galleys landed a body of raiders in 1595, when Penzance, Mousehole, and Newlyn were burnt. Falmouth may have been saved only by gales from an attack in 1597, for it was reported to the Privy Council that Pendennis Castle was unfit to repel troops should they land. By February 1598 four hundred men had been set to labour there under supervision of Paul Ivey, and in August 1599

9

over a hundred were still employed. Round the headland they had built walls with embrasures for cannon and in front of them a steep stone-revetted ditch, well seen today from Castle Drive. Yet to be erected was the outer gateway in these defences; this Italianate feature was completed probably at the end of 1611.

Killigrew is a name constantly occurring in local annals and usually linked with turbulence. It was borne by several who held the office of governor of Pendennis which was not finally abolished until 1837. The first of these, John Killigrew, was requisitioning "serpentine powder" in 1546, as soon as he was appointed. A son (knighted) and grandson, both John, followed him in the post, enjoying fortune, enduring disgrace. A more celebrated man among the governors was Sir Peter Killigrew, founder of the fortunes of modern Falmouth. Before his time the locality, called Smithwick, was occupied merely by his seat, Arwenack Manor, and a few fishermen's huts. Sir Peter obtained privileges of markets and fairs, and lastly from Charles the Second in 1661 a charter of incorporation under the name Falmouth. He had been chosen as governor by General Monck in the previous March, and as he was a Royalist and the Restoration was yet two months away, the politicians gossiped. At the end of this long connexion of family with castle, this "fascinating history of imprisonments, escapes, dubious dealings at sea", it was a Killigrew heir, Sir John Wodehouse, from whom the Crown purchased the Pendennis headland in 1795.

As far as its occupants were concerned, the history of Pendennis seems to have been mostly a tale of tribulation and neglect. The garrison varied widely in numbers. Carew, for instance, reported that in 1599 there were 80 musketeers, 60 pikemen, and 60 armed with calivers – these last were ponderous hand-guns, fired from a rest. In 1626 the defenders were said to be two years in arrear with pay and living on limpets. Some indeed perished for want. In eleven years there were 69 petitions to Westminster for more humane treatment. The Civil War was one exciting episode; indeed the siege of this castle was important nationally. It was held for Charles the First by Colonel John Arundell, of Trerice, nicknamed "Jack-for-the-King" and also "Old Tilbury" because he had been present when Elizabeth the First reviewed her troops at Tilbury in 1588. Appointed governor in 1643, he was probably over seventy.

Fairfax, marching into Cornwall with the Parliamentary army while Royalist Exeter was still invested, arrived in the neighbourhood on 18

*Air view, looking west*

March 1646, snatched the fort on Dennis Head at the mouth of Helford River, and summoned the aged governor of Pendennis to surrender the castle. Arundell's reply has been immortalised in the State Papers collected by Clarendon for his history of the Civil War. It included: "I will here bury myself before I deliver up this castle to such as fight against his Majesty" – a promise not exactly made good. The men Arundell commanded were described as "blades of the right stamp", who "spare not to be daily drunk, and this the governor encourages". They kept fires all night, according to Sprigge, and "were very prodigall of their powder, making two hundred great shot in the space of three dayes at our men". The place was besieged on the ground by Colonels Fortescue and Hammond, and blockaded from the sea by Captain Batten, in the *St. Andrews*, who also had "ten large boats and barges" watching the harbour by night. Supplies of food and ammunition shipped to the besieged from St. Malo could not be landed. In July, Arundell sent Prince Charles a message that they could not hold out many days without relief. Some of the garrison burst out in search of supplies. Their boats were beaten back. At last, on 17 August, they hauled down the flag to Colonel Richard

Townsend and were granted full honours of war, marching out with "flying colours, trumpets sounding, drums beating, matches lighted at both ends, bullets in their mouths, and every soldier twelve charges of powder". Twenty-four officers and some 900 other survivors came forth. But so famished and feeble were they that several died soon after regaling themselves. Only Raglan, of castles in England, by two days, resisted longer. How Parliament had been worried may be judged from its appointment of 22 September as a day of thanksgiving for the reduction of Pendennis among other obstacles.

Distinguished visitors came to the castle at that period. In July 1644, Queen Henrietta Maria spent one night on her way from Exeter, where her baby daughter was left, before sailing to France. She might have met the Duke of Hamilton, a prisoner for some eighteen months on suspicion of disloyalty to the Royal cause; certainly Clarendon had a long interview with him here in August 1645. The future Charles the Second stayed next year from 13 February to 2 March, but he was away for Scilly before the siege set in. Political offenders to undergo terms of imprisonment were Colonel Edward Hervey, a regicide; William Prynne, the pamphleteer;

*The circular curtain wall is well seen from the west*

*Little Dennis in decay*

Sir John Wildman, "plotter and postmaster". The last captives were French soldiers taken at the battle of Corunna in 1809.

On the jagged rocks below and to the south-east of the castle is a blockhouse whose popular name was Little Dennis. It appears to have been remodelled about 1540 from a fort a few years older, and was dismantled in 1654. Pendennis Castle was badly damaged by lightning in 1717 and not fully repaired until about thirty years later when affairs abroad made it desirable for the fort to be put again in a state of defence. At various dates buildings were added for purposes residential or military: barracks, armoury, magazine, the Crab Quay and Half Moon batteries.

But that part of the monument which visitors go round today consists of the inner fortress of 1543 enclosed within the late Elizabethan enceinte of between three and four acres with angular bastions, and the shell of Little Dennis. Its main entrance is through a gate in the outer defences on the north-west side. Towards the south-east end of the enclosure will be found the keep.

This is a circular tower of three storeys, 35 feet high and 56 feet in diameter, surrounded by what has been called a low chemise, or a curtain

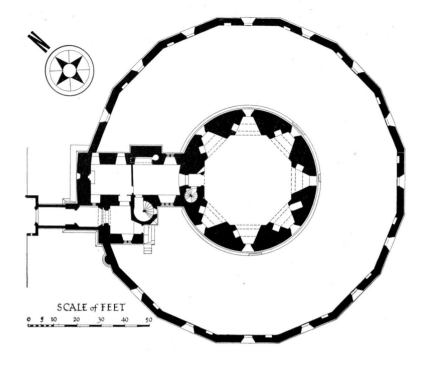

SCALE of FEET

0  5  10    20    30    40    50

wall ringed by a fosse, this last a dry ditch. All its materials are local stone; the keep is of granite ashlar with freestone from Pentewan for carvings, and the curtain wall is chiefly of shale.

The principal entrance to the keep is approached by a drawbridge on one arch over the ditch, and was originally protected by a portcullis. About 100 years ago the War Office, deeming the drawbridge no longer safe, built the present permanent footway over its stone supports, and for the last time pulled up the portcullis, which is preserved intact except for the iron points that shod its wooden uprights. Over the door, carved in relief on a rectangular stone panel set in the masonry, is the sole external ornament of the keep, unless gargoyles for rain water be allowed. This device portrays the Royal Arms, the leopards of England quartered by French lilies and supported by the Tudor lion and dragon, with the motto DIEU ET MON DROIT below, the whole framed by a raised moulding adorned with a conventional pattern of foliage.

Through this door the visitor passes, as he often does at a castle, into

*The entrance gateway*

the first floor of the keep, to find himself in an octagonal room with walls 16 feet thick. He may descend a spiral staircase one flight to the dark chamber in the basement which is the same shape and served as the kitchen. The same staircase, and a wider, easier one outside the octagonal room, both go up to the top floor where most of the interesting features may be examined. Here the garrison worked the mechanism of their defences. In a chamber on the left-hand side of the entrance to this floor are two long slits through which the chains of the drawbridge passed to the hand-winch (now disappeared), and on either side of these slits are narrow channels in the wall through which ran the ropes of the portcullis. Here also were living quarters, according to tradition the lodging of Prince Charles.

The gun ports of the fortress deserve attention; they are splayed inwards and outwards to allow a wide traverse of the guns, and furnished with smoke vents. The pieces were made from iron and brass, mounted on wooden carriages, and the balls they fired were of stone or cast iron. An idea of the ordnance will be suggested by a note in the historical section on St. Mawes. Since much of the stone shot excavated in the vicinity of

*Going into the keep*

*Inside the keep*

Pendennis is bigger than the $5\frac{1}{2}$-inch ball fired by the heaviest gun named, probably cannon were mounted also. The men would arm themselves with pikes, bills, muskets, or calivers.

From the leads of the keep on a clear day the visitor takes in a magnificent view of the surrounding country including Falmouth and St. Mawes, Carrick Roads, and glimpses of coastline from the Dodman to the Manacles. In the middle of the roof rises a little octagonal look-out turret with glass windows, and to the north a tinier stair turret, both embattled. A powder magazine with space for at least 240 barrels used to stand on the leads.

To inspect the curtain wall the way is through a wooden door immediately opposite the main entrance giving on to what was formerly a flagged wall walk but is now a grassy circle. Gun ports of the curtain were devised similarly to those of the keep, with inward and outward splay. We can imagine the defenders of 1646 firing their heavy guns through the embrasures in this curtain.

## Typical cannon of Tudor times

*Top,* long culverin *(from the* ZEUGBUCH *of Emperor Maximilian* I*); middle,*
*Pevensey gun; bottom,* "Mons Meg" *(Edinburgh Castle)*

*As seen by the Bucks more than 200 years ago*

# St. Mawes Castle

This name is one of various spellings of that of a saint who came from Wales and founded here a holy well. The first we hear about a castle is a report in 1540 by Thomas Treffry, the King's Clerk of Works here, that he is about to go to Falmouth "for setting out the fortlett on the east side of the entry of the Haven".

Compared with Pendennis, St. Mawes has a history almost void of colour, calling for little to be related beyond the names of a few governors. Many of these quarrelled with or intrigued against their opposite numbers across the inlet; any idea of friendly rivalry is missing. First of the line, nominated in 1544, was Michael Vyvyan, of the family who still hold the estate of Trelowarren at the head of Helford River. His successor from 1561, Hannibal Vyvyan, enjoyed a long tenure: he it was who sent to Drake in London news of the Spanish raid on Penzance in 1595, and there exists at Trelowarren Park today a bell cast for his use at the castle, stamped with a crowned fleur-de-lys and inscribed "Hanniball Vivian 1600". He was followed in office from 1603 by Sir Francis Vyvyan, who in 1632 was tried and cashiered by the Star Chamber for "practising a variety of deceptions". When the Civil War broke out, the governor was a scion of

19

*Air view, looking east*

another well-known Cornish family, Hannibal Bonython. Reasonably enough, if incredibly for one with that first name, he decided that those who put this castle on the slope of a hill meant that it was to protect the harbour only and could not be held against an assault from the landward side; so when Fairfax led up his army on 12 March 1646 only a brief parley was required, neither gunfire nor bloodshed, before the place capitulated. That was the only action it ever saw. Later governors, Sir Joseph Tredinham and Sir George Nugent, sat in Parliament as Members for St. Mawes. It kept the right to return Members from 1572 until the Reform Act of 1832 abolished "rotten boroughs". The office of governor endured till 1849. At one time the land was owned by the Dukes of Buckingham, from whom it passed as Crown property.

But though political or romantic events are few, some military statistics enliven the records. We learn that the normal garrison of St. Mawes in the early decades varied between 100 in 1599 and 16 (including the governor

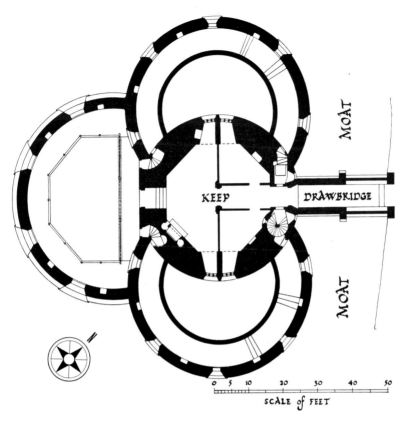

KEEP

DRAWBRIDGE

MOAT

MOAT

0 5 10 20 30 40 50

SCALE of FEET

and lieutenant) in 1636, when daily pay was 3s. for the governor, 1s. 6d. for the lieutenant, a shilling apiece for two gunners, and eightpence each for the others. Their number would be raised in times of danger by men "pressed" in neighbouring parishes, who brought their own pikes and muskets. A survey of the ordnance taken in 1609 mentions two sakers and an iron minion on the roof, a culverin and six demi-culverins of iron and one of brass on the bastions, two culverins and a brass saker in the court-yards. The calibre of a minion was $3\frac{1}{4}$ inches and its weight 1,100 – 1,200 pounds (about half a ton); of a saker, $3\frac{1}{2}$ inches and 1,500 pounds; of a demi-culverin, 4 inches and 3,000 pounds; of a culverin, $5\frac{1}{2}$ inches and 4,000 pounds (nearly two tons). Another survey in 1623 alludes to a culverin on a wooden carriage on the roof, and a second on the roof over the southern courtyard; it also reveals that the defences included two earthworks built outside the east and west curtain walls. On the castle being surrendered in

1646 the captured armament amounted to thirteen pieces of ordnance and 160 small-arms.

Much more compact than its twin, St. Mawes Castle consists primarily of a low round central tower, called for convenience the keep, within three semicircular bastions, or lunettes, with emplacements for eleven heavy guns arranged about it in clover-leaf plan. The nicest simile is an ace of clubs. To Dr. Pevsner this trefoil pattern gives "an impression of all-round symmetry and harmony of composition strikingly unmedieval and convincingly of the Renaissance". In the eyes of Dr. A. L. Rowse (as, earlier, for Oman) St. Mawes is of all Henry the Eighth's buildings the most decorative. Again the materials are local shale with occasional granite and freestone worked in. The keep, four storeys high if one counts a small turret with cupola, rises 44 feet from base to parapet, and is said to reach exactly 100 feet above high-water level. The craggy harshness of the eminence it stands on is softened in season by a spread of mesembryanthemum, rock plants, and tropical shrubs almost down to the water's edge. Below the castle on the rocks are a Tudor blockhouse with four gun ports, and a magazine and further emplacements of last century.

Approach to the main entrance of the keep is on the north-east or landward side, through a hexagonal guard-house and then across a two-

*Flowering shrubs against background of stone delight the summer visitor*

*Bridge and entrance gateway*

arched stone bridge with wooden planking over a deep dry ditch. There was originally a drawbridge working on chains that ran through the two long narrow slits over the archway. It was as usual overlooked by cross-slits for musketry fire cut in the keep wall on either side. The Royal Arms on the tower face are precisely like those described under Pendennis; but higher up, carved on the string course girdling the keep below the battlements, is something quite new and an example of the feature for which St. Mawes is chiefly noted. This is the first in a series of inscriptions of Latin hexameters composed at the request of the King's Clerk of Works by John Leland, Chaplain and Antiquary to His Majesty. It offers a confident prologue to a tour of the castle: SEMPER HONOS HENRICE TUUS LAUDESQUE MANEBUNT (Henry, thy honour and praises will remain for ever).

On walking through the doorway the visitor enters the first floor of the keep. Other floors and the rampart walks of the bastions are reached by stone staircases. At the foot of the right-hand flight, behind the fine oak door, is a rather startling deep square shaft under a trap; it terminates in a shallow alcove holding a stone seat. Over the doorways of the first two rooms in the corridor ahead are sixteenth-century carvings. The right-hand archway contains the Tudor rose and fleur-de-lys; that on the left is ornamented with two shields bearing fleurs-de-lys and wreathed in carved

*Original carvings over doorways*

*The Royal Arms between Tritons holding a scroll*

foliage from which peep the heads of a monk and a cherub. Over the wider door half-way down the corridor is some coarser work of the same period, two scrolls within and two without carrying the words "God save King Henry the Eighth" and "God save Prince Edward", and four heads, one a good portrait of a soldier wearing a morion or steel helmet.

From the largest room on this floor a stepped arch leads to the southern bastion. This is battlemented, the square openings between the battlements being socketed for light guns. Square recesses in the wall were for small shot. On this side of the keep are four small carved shields, two framed in the Garter, and a large square panel containing the Royal Arms in low relief. All shields are blank through erosion by weather. Left and right of the panel two Tritons hold a scroll with the inscription SEMPER VIVET ANIMA REGIS HENRICI OCTAVI QUI ANNO 34 SUI RENGNI HOC FECIT FIERI (May the soul live for ever of Henry the Eighth who had this made in the thirty-fourth year of his reign).

Arches and stairs lead to the lateral bastions, each of which has five embrasures socketed for light guns. Grooves will be observed in the tops of the battlements on either side of each embrasure; they were for the hinges

*Entrance passage,
looking south*

of the mantlets, wooden shutters hung across for protection of the gunners. The rampart walk of the eastern bastion returns to the main stair of the keep. One next ascends to an octagonal room called in old surveys the gun room. On the stone platform immediately inside its door once stood the winch of the drawbridge, and chain-slits can be seen in the wall below the window. Each of the eight recesses in the room has its ammunition cupboard and smoke vent. The gun ports have been glazed; the roof and wooden benches are also modern.

Another flight of steps goes up to the battlemented roof and a small turret. Though this when a watch-tower may have been flat-topped and battlemented, it was almost entirely rebuilt in the seventeenth century, and most of the windows have been filled in.

In the basement of the keep is a stone-paved kitchen. At the left-hand side of the fireplace, bread was baked in a brick-lined oven. The granite pillars supporting the roof are original, as are some beams. Facing the entrance is a curious carved pedestal; it may have supported a brass or pewter basin for washing, the ewer being hung in the niche behind.

On the next floor up, the ancient mess-room of the garrison shows a fine granite chimney-piece. The recess over the mantelshelf is designed for a carved panel, probably heraldic, but long since missing. Part of the composition is hidden by the ceiling erected about 1880 when the castle was partitioned to make extra accommodation for married quarters. Another Tudor fireplace can be found nearby; the square recess in the chimney at the right is called a salt-box, as salt was customarily stored in such places to keep it dry. In the wall across the mess-room a quatrefoil-shaped opening was cut to command the staircase.

Another stepped arch leads from the mess-room to the courtyards of the bastions, which formed the lowest battery. The walls are pierced by eleven casemates for large cannon with smoke vents over each. Some embrasures show traces of shutters, and all have sockets for the beams that bolted the shutters home. The two last openings in the lateral courtyards face into the ditch under the drawbridge and are filled with musketry slots, since powerful guns were not needed there. The central courtyard was originally roofed; the stone corbels supporting the beams are still visible under the wooden balcony and at the angles of the masonry opposite.

No one should miss the gardens and lawns, to which access may be gained through one of the gun ports. The exterior walls of the castle are

*The eight-sided gun room*

adorned by three unfinished Royal arms and three more of Leland's inscriptions. The western bastion, facing up the Fal, bears EDWARDUS FAMA REFERAT FACTISQUE PARENTEM (May Edward resemble his father in fame and deeds). On the south we read HONORA HENRICUM OCTAVUM ANGLIE FRANCIE ET HIBERNIE REGEM EXCELLENTISSIMUM (Honour Henry the Eighth, most excellent king of England, France, and Ireland). And GAUDEAT EDWARDO NUNC DUCE CORNUBIA FELIX (Let fortunate Cornwall rejoice that Edward is now her Duke), exclaims the eastern wall. (The scansion requires DUCE NUNC and that is what Leland wrote, but the carver produced the version quoted). Apart from these adornments, it is the boast of St. Mawes that few ancient monuments in Britain can claim gardens with more gaiety and variety in what they grow.

*The south bastion honours the founder in Latin verse*

Printed in England for Her Majesty's Stationery Office
by Eyre and Spottiswoode Limited at Grosvenor Press Portsmouth

Dd.501327 K162 9/70